Is The Tomb of King Tut Really Cursed?

History Books for Kids 4th Grade

Children's Ancient History

In this book, we're going to talk about King Tut's tomb and whether it was cursed or not. So, let's get right to it!

After Egyptian pharaohs died, and were buried for their crossover into the afterlife, tomb raiders have broken into their tombs to steal the treasures that had been placed there. At one point, in the early 1900s, archaeologists believed that there were no more treasures to find. However, the persistence of one man proved that they were wrong.

Valley of the Kings

WHERE WAS KING TUTANKHAMUN'S TOMB?

For almost 500 years, from a period of time spanning from the 16th century to the 11 century BC, the Valley of the Kings, in what is now Luxor, Egypt, was where the Egyptians buried their dead pharaohs. The pharaohs and influential nobles of the New Kingdom were buried there in tombs that were cut from rocks.

By 1914, many of the teams exploring in the area felt that any remaining tombs had already been found. However, one archaeologist, Howard Carter, didn't agree with that assessment. He felt strongly that a very important tomb had not yet been found. It was the tomb of Tutankhamun or King Tut for short.

Statue of Akhenaten

WHO WAS KING TUT?

Tutankhaten, which was his original name, was born around 1341 BC, over 3,350 years ago. He was the son of the controversial Pharaoh Akhenaten. Akhenaten

Had attempted to get the Egyptian citizens to change their religion. Tut's father wanted Egypt to worship Aten, the sun disc. The Egyptians had many gods and goddesses and Akhenaten began to destroy the images of these other deities so that the people would follow what he wanted.

Pharaoh Akhenaten

Queen Nefertiti

$H$is wife, the beautiful Queen Nefertiti, supported her husband's beliefs. Queen Nefertiti was Akhenaten's main wife, and historians believe that she wasn't the mother of Tutankhaten, but this isn't known with 100% certainty.

When Tutankhaten was only 9 years old, his father died and he took the throne of Egypt. He would have needed the support of advisers since he was so young. It's not known when this happened, but he eventually changed the last four letters of his name so that it wasn't associated with the god "Aten." He was then called Tutankhamun, with the last four letters of his name corresponding to "Amun," the god that the Egyptians called "the main god of all the gods."

Amun Temple

King Tut Burial Mask

Tut condemned the religious changes that his father and Nefertiti had made and went back to the former religious beliefs. Unfortunately, King Tut had very poor health. He was only 18 years old when he died, and evidence at the tomb has led historians to believe that his death was unexpected.

WHO FOUND KING TUTANKHAMUN'S TOMB?

✧✧✧✧✧✧✧✧✧✧✧✧✧✧✧✧✧✧✧✧✧✧

Howard Carter was convinced he could find Tut's tomb, but his investor Lord Carnarvon was becoming frustrated with Carter's lack of progress. After all, it took a lot of money to make it possible for Carter to keep searching and this expedition had gone on for years.

Chair from tomb of Tutankhamun

Carter had been exploring for five years and had nothing to show for his efforts. Finally, Lord Carnarvon told Carter that he would only give him funding for one more year. Carter was under stress. King Tut's tomb was out there. He knew he had to find it.

Then, something happened that changed everything. Carter had been looking for about six years when in 1922 he found a hidden step under some laborers' huts. He started to dig and found a stairway and then a door. When they got into the tomb, Carter and his workers could hardly believe their eyes.

King Tutankhamun's tomb in Valley of the Kings, Egypt

Inside the small tomb, which was only about 1100 square feet, were thousands of precious items. There were 3,000 individual objects ranging from King Tut's gold-masked coffin to chariots to jewelry and amulets. Many of the items were made of gold and silver and decorated with precious gems. They quickly realized that they had found one of the most amazing discoveries in all of archaeological history.

HOW BIG WAS THE TOMB?

ost tombs designed for Pharaohs were much larger than Tut's tomb. Archaeologists think that this is because his death was unexpected. The tomb may have been meant for someone else, such as an influential nobleman, but had to be used for Tut when he died, because a tomb hadn't been prepared for him yet due to his age.

Tutankhamun's bed

The small tomb had four different rooms. The antechamber was the first room that Carter entered. The contents weren't placed in an organized way. The antechamber was piled with furniture that was covered in gold and chariots that were dismantled.

The burial chamber held the King's coffin, called a sarcophagus. The sarcophagus had three coffins that were nested inside each other, with the boy-Pharaoh's mummy inside the innermost coffin. The coffin that held his mummy was made of solid gold. The room also contained King Tut's gold death mask, which is probably the most well known of all the artifacts.

Pharaoh Sarcophagus

Canopic Jars

The treasury had a golden shrine with jars containing his bodily organs. These jars are called canopic jars. There were also elaborate statues as well as model boats.

The annex contained more furniture and also contained jars of oils and precious ointments. There was food and wine for the young Pharaoh to eat on his journey to the afterlife. There were even board games so the Pharaoh would have something to amuse himself during his trip.

There were so many items that it took Carter's team over 10 years to catalog and properly annotate everything that they had found. They had uncovered a treasure that was worth many millions of dollars and was priceless in terms of the historical knowledge of the New Kingdom and the ancient culture of Egypt.

Many of these valuable treasures have been around the world and displayed in various museums.

WAS THERE REALLY A CURSE ON THOSE WHO OPENED THE TOMB?

As soon as the tomb was opened, there were stories that circulated saying that whoever violated the tomb would die an untimely death. A few of the individuals that were involved in the opening of the tomb did die not long after it was opened, so the legend of the curse gained steam after that.

Howard Carter und Lord Carnarvon

The very first legend was that Howard Carter's pet canary had succumbed to a cobra on the very day the tomb was opened. Carter had brought the bird with him to Egypt and when he got home that evening, his servant met him at the door with a few yellow feathers.

He was terrified and told Carter that the Pharaoh's sacred serpent had killed the bird because the bird had helped Carter to find his tomb. Carter was upset that the bird had been killed and made sure that the dangerous cobra was out of the house, but he was a practical man and didn't believe in superstitions.

Golden bust of King Tut

The day the tomb was opened there was a huge celebration. No one seemed concerned about a curse. Later, rumors circulated that Carter had found a tablet with the curse inscribed on it, but he denied that such a tablet ever existed.

THE PRESS PERPETRATES THE RUMOR

A few months after the tomb was opened, the next tragedy struck. Lord Carnarvon who had come to Egypt to witness the tomb's opening got very sick from an infection that started with a mosquito bite on his cheek. Legend says that the lights in Cairo went out when he died and back in England his son reported that at that precise time the Lord's favorite dog howled in anguish.

The press was intrigued when in 1925 King Tut's mummy was unveiled. It had a wound positioned on the left cheek in the same place that Lord Carnarvon's had been! By 1929, more than ten people who were somehow connected with the discovery of the tomb had passed away from unnatural causes.

Two of Lord Carnarvon's relatives as well as Richard Bethell, who was Carter's personal secretary, and Lord Westbury who was Bethell's father had all died. Filled with grief over his son's death, Westbury jumped off a building to kill himself. He left a suicide note stating that he couldn't "tolerate any more horrors."

This was a sensational series of events and the press jumped on every item as they announced that the tomb was truly cursed by Tut's mummy. By 1935, over 20 deaths had been attached to the tomb's opening.

In 2002, a scholar by the name of Mark Nelson did an analysis of all the people associated with the tomb and found the death rate to be no higher than death rates in any normal population.

The story about Howard Carter's canary and the power failure in Cairo were both fabricated and untrue. In fact, some people believe that Carter started the curse rumor himself to ensure that the treasures

in the tomb weren't stolen. After all, if they had been, the world would never have seen these glorious artifacts of Egypt and the discovery that he had spent many years of his life trying to achieve.

Awesome! Now you know more about King Tut's tomb and the alleged curse of King Tut. You can find more Ancient History books from Baby Professor by searching the website of your favorite book retailer.

Visit
BABY PROFESSOR
EDUCATION KIDS
www.BabyProfessorBooks.com
to download Free Baby Professor eBooks and view
our catalog of new and exciting Children's Books